1959

1960

1965

1963

ISABEL PIN

I Am Coco

The Life of COCO CHANEL

PRESTEL
Munich · London · New York

Contents

Introduction 8

Little Coco 10

A wandering family 12

Farewell to Mom 14

Alone 16

The orphanage 18

Sewing is fun! 20

Real life 22

Applause! Applause! 24

A chateau for Coco 26

A woman in trousers 28

Feeling free 30

Ooh la la, love! 32

Paris, at last! 34

A breath of fresh air in fashion 36

Sailor look 38

Coco the rebel 40

At war 42

Fashion house on the Atlantic 44

The sewing machines never stop 46

Away with ponytails! 48

'CC': the brand 50

A broken heart   52

Journey to Venice   54

Among friends   56

Darling Coco   58

Villa with a sea view   60

31 Rue Cambon   62

Hello, Coco   66

All women are Chanel   68

Jewelry is chic   70

War, again   72

In exile   74

Coco is back   76

The most famous perfume   78

The quilted bag   80

The 'little black dress'   82

Farewell, Coco   84

Chanel forever   86

Spectacular shows   88

Catwalks   90

Biography   92

"My life didn't please me,
so I created my life."

COCO CHANEL

Have you heard of Coco Chanel?

Coco created a new style using innovative fabrics and concepts: designing hats, jackets, dresses and slacks. She also developed her own perfume, a handbag and jewelry. She became world famous.

This book tells the story of Coco Chanel. It's the adventure of a brave girl, who was determined to become a strong and independent woman. And she did just that. *Chapeau, Coco!*

Little Coco

Coco Chanel was born on a summer's day on August 19, 1883, in Saumur, an old town on the French river Loire. She was baptized by the name of Gabrielle.

Her mother, Jeanne Devolle, came from a poor background. Jeanne and her older brother, Marin, her only sibling, were looked after by their uncle Augustin. When Jeanne met Albert Chanel as a teenager, she fell madly in love with him. Jeanne had no work and had never left her village, so a life with the adventurer Albert had to be exciting! Jeanne was only 19 years old when Gabrielle was born.

Gabrielle's father, Albert, also came from a poor family. But unlike Jeanne, he had lots of brothers and sisters—18 to be exact! Just like his own father, Albert was a peddler. He traveled from town to town with a cart and sold his goods at fairs: fabrics, wine, sausages and much, much more. Albert had jet black hair and a moustache, talked a lot and liked to please the ladies. But above all, he liked to do what he wanted. When he met Jeanne, he was not keen on giving up his freedom.

A wandering family

Gabrielle had five brothers and sisters: the older Julia-Berthe and the younger Alphonse, Antoinette, Lucien and Augustin, the last of whom died shortly after his birth.

Father Albert spent very little time with the family, so mother Jeanne had to look after the children and the home. Money was always tight.

Gabrielle and her siblings liked living in the countryside near Coupière, in the west of France. They lived a happy life, attending school, playing games and going fishing. They gathered blackberries and mushrooms in the woods, and they loved gardening with their great uncle Augustin.

Farewell
to Mom

Mother Jeanne grew tired. She was often alone, and running a home needs a lot of energy. One day, she fell ill. It was far more difficult at that time to get treatment for sickness, and Jeanne became worse and worse. When she died in 1895, Gabrielle was just eleven years old.

Because father Albert did not want to look after his children, he had his two sons taken in by a farmer's family. There, they slept with the animals in a barn and had to work all day. Albert took the three daughters, Julia, Gabrielle and Antoinette, in his cart to an orphanage in Aubazine, about an hour away.

Alone

Albert dropped his daughters off at the gate of the orphanage in
Aubazine. He said his goodbyes and returned to his life as a wanderer
on the country roads. On seeing her father drive off, Gabrielle began
to cry bitterly. She didn't know if she would ever see him again.

The orphanage

The orphanage was a convent run by nuns. Life there was hard for the three girls. Their large, cold dormitory had iron beds with uncomfortable straw mattresses. There was just one wash basin with no toilet. And for meals, they usually ate vegetable soup with croutons, which did not taste very good at all.

The children had lessons in the morning. Afterwards, they had to clean, wash and cook. The nuns also made sure that everyone prayed regularly. Gabrielle, however, had a bit of luck—she learned to sew in the orphanage, which was something she came to enjoy.

The best times of the year were holidays! Gabrielle spent them with her aunt Adrienne, who was just a little bit older than her. While staying with Adrienne, Gabrielle began to learn about fashion. She loved dresses and hats! Adrienne and Gabrielle bought hat molds, or wooden blocks carved into the shape of a hat. They would then use the molds to make hats, which they would decorate using a lot of imagination.

Sewing is fun!

Shortly before her 18th birthday, Gabrielle had to leave the convent because she was too old. She moved to the Notre-Dame boarding school in Moulins, in the Auvergne region, where her aunt Adrienne also lived.

Gabrielle dreamt of freedom, but she also wanted to finish her education. Her passion was sewing, and there was so much to learn: cutting, stitching, embroidering, ironing, unpicking and then starting off all over again. Gabrielle plugged away and never gave up. It made her happy when she could finish a dress, an apron or a jacket—and Aunt Adrienne tried on everything!

"To achieve great things,
we must first dream."
COCO CHANEL

Real life

Two years later, Gabrielle had had enough of convents and boarding schools! She and Adrienne found work together at 'Saint Marie—Silk, Laces and Ribbons' in Moulins. They lived in a room above this elegant store and remained the best of friends.

Neither of them owned more than two dresses, two aprons and a couple of blouses, but on Sundays they wore hats—usually a small, flat, straw boater hat, known as the 'canotier', which they carefully stored in a round box. Their food was always the same, namely bread, cheese and vegetable broth. They were poor but didn't care. They looked forward to the future and enjoyed their life in the heart of the town. There was so much more going on in their lives than before!

Applause! Applause!

Many French army officers were stationed in the garrison town of Moulins. They were nicknamed 'mustachios' and liked to have fun in their free time. They often invited Adrienne and Gabrielle to the Rotonde, which was a popular venue with a variety theater. There they would sit at small marble tables and sip beer, lemonade squash or champagne while musicians performed.

Gabrielle was always getting new ideas, and she decided in 1904 to try her luck on the stage. Her sassy song about a missing dog named Coco became especially popular!

In an enthusiastic chorus, the audience chanted 'Coco, Coco!', as if that were Gabrielle's name. And because she liked the name, that was what she called herself from then on. Coco Chanel—it was the name of a young woman full of courage and energy!

A chateau for Coco

At the Rotonde, Coco met Étienne Balsan. He was a young officer and liked Coco very much. He invited her to live with him at his estate north of Paris, which had a chateau and a large horse farm.

Life at the chateau was fun, with parties full of laughter, discussion and dancing. Étienne and Coco often went riding together, because Étienne was hugely passionate about horses.

A woman in trousers

Life at the chateau was something completely new for Coco.
She grew to love luxury and always got up late. It was so enjoyable
to read romantic novels in bed! And when she began to get bored,
she decided to learn how to ride a horse. In those days, women
in long skirts sat sideways on the horse, or 'side-saddle'.
Coco, however, found this method extremely uncomfortable.
She wanted to ride like a man—in trousers!

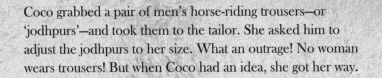

Coco grabbed a pair of men's horse-riding trousers—or 'jodhpurs'—and took them to the tailor. She asked him to adjust the jodhpurs to her size. What an outrage! No woman wears trousers! But when Coco had an idea, she got her way.

Wearing her new riding outfit, she climbed on to the horse and learned how to walk, trot and canter! Coco became a very good rider, boldly and courageously impressing everyone.

Feeling free

Coco rummaged through the whole chateau and gathered up assorted men's clothing. She cut and recut. She shortened slacks and shirts and transformed everything into a practical wardrobe for herself. Women should be able to move as freely as men!

Trousers for women!

They go well with fine ankle boots or elegant riding boots.

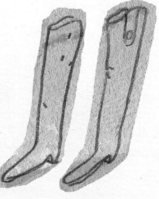

The 'canotier':
a light straw hat with
a narrow brim.

Cravats for riders
are worn knotted
or long.

*"Beauty begins
the moment you decide
to be yourself."*

COCO CHANEL

The blouse has
short sleeves
and no frills.

Ooh la la, love!

One day, Arthur Capel arrived as a guest of Étienne. Everyone just called him 'Boy'. Coco soon fell head over heels in love with this handsome Englishman. He had green eyes, black hair and incredible charm. Boy came from a wealthy and educated family, and he would become Coco's partner and accomplice. He supported her in everything she had planned. Boy was Coco's great love!

Paris, at last!

Life in the chateau was very comfortable, but it wasn't enough for Coco. She wanted to be independent and earn her own money. To do this, she had to take her life into her own hands.

Brave Coco! She threw herself into the adventure and moved to Paris, the very city of style and elegance. Here she opened her first fashion store for elegant hats, and she quickly enjoyed success. All the fine ladies flocked to 21 Rue Cambon to buy at Chanel!

A breath of fresh air in fashion

On a weekend by the sea with Boy, Coco discovered Deauville, a posh seaside resort in northern France. This was where she wanted to open a boutique, right on the colorful beach promenade! And Boy would help her.

Coco sold dresses in Deauville that made women feel light and free.
They no longer had to be constrained by tight, stiff corsets. Her customers
loved the new lightness of the cuts and fabrics. Dressed in Chanel, they
could even relax on the beach!

Sailor look

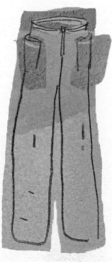

Coco Chanel's creations around
1914 were simple, yet elegant.
She was inspired by the clothing
of fishermen and sailors on
the coast.

Striped sailor blouses
could be worn with wide
slacks and flowing skirts.

Cardigans and berets: in Coco's day,
these were clothes worn by country folk.
Coco turned them into timeless and
ultra-modern fashion items.

All the ladies
loved Chanel's
light tunic dresses.

Coco Chanel did what she wanted and lived how she wanted! She not only designed clothing, she also created a whole new lifestyle. Coco didn't need to rely on a husband. In her long slacks and knee-length skirts, she ran her own life. She drove her own car and ran her own fashion business.

Coco, the rebel

"I decided who I wanted to be and that is who I am."

COCO CHANEL

Seldom before had a woman been so bold. Coco showed the women of her day that being a woman meant being brave, free and independent.

At war

World War I erupted in the summer of 1914, and went on for four long years. All the men had to take part in the war, whether they lived in the countryside or the city, and whether they were poor or rich. And the women? They took care of the wounded and worked in canteen kitchens. They even worked in factories making weapons.

Coco also adapted. She remembered the simple, rough-cloth uniforms she had to wear as a child in the orphanage. She used these memories to create similar gowns for nurses.

Despite the war, Coco opened a large, modern store with her own sensational collection in Biarritz. She sold expensive, tailor-made fashion items.

Fashion house on the Atlantic

And because the city of Biarritz was in the south of France, not far from the Spanish border, both French and Spanish customers flocked to Coco Chanel.

The sewing machines never stopped

Coco began ordering her fabrics
from nearby Spain, which was
not in the war. She also designed
dresses from flowing fabrics.
These included jersey fabrics,
which were a new type of
material. Coco loved the lightness of the material. And around
the waist she could wrap a simple
scarf—super convenient!

Coco was on the go around
the clock and her tasks were
many. She had to pick out
colors and create cuts. She
considered new designs and
elaborate embroidery, as well
as everything from the types
of buttons to the fastenings.
Sixty seamstresses worked
for her.

Away with ponytails!

Life changed radically during wartime, for both men and women. Many men died in the war and women had to make do without them. Women became more active, self-confident and independent.

Coco's designs and lifestyle fit perfectly with these times. Dresses from Chanel allowed women to feel comfortable and move more freely.

With this feeling of liberation and ease at the back of her mind, Coco took a large pair of scissors and lopped off her long, black ponytail. Once again, Coco shaped a whole new fashion style, one that was boyish and free. Her new look, called the 'garçonne', was admired everywhere!

'CC': the brand

Coco designed her very own trademark.

According to legend, she discovered her 'CC' logo
in Aubazine—in the window of the chapel at the
orphanage. Gabrielle would often pray there as a child.

The two 'C's, of course, were her name's initials,
and she intertwined them artistically in the
trademark image.

"There is a time for work
and a time for love.
That leaves no other time."

COCO CHANEL

A broken heart

Coco was very attached to her friend, Boy. He was everything in one for her: friend, confidant, lover and business partner. However, on a December day in 1919, he suddenly died in a car accident.

This tragedy broke Coco's heart. She covered all the walls and the ceiling of her bedroom in black fabric. She even had the window frames and shutters painted black. This color reflected the deep sadness that she carried within her.

Journey to Venice

Coco was not alone in her grief, as her very close friend Misia stayed at her side. Misia was fun-loving, adored art and took Coco with her to Italy. Coco was relieved to be doing something new. The old frescoes and famous Italian architecture brought color back into her life. She couldn't get enough of Venice, with its canals, its lagoon and its art.

All of these sights would influence her later designs. Coco was particularly impressed by the lions—the symbolic animal of Venice—that adorned many Venetian houses. The lion would soon become her own symbol of strength.

Among friends

Dmitri Pavlovich
Grand Duke and champagne seller

Serge Diaghilev
Art critic

Coco Cha

Igor Stravinsky
Composer

Jean Cocteau
Writer

Pablo Picass
Painter and sculptor

Pierre Reverdy
Poet

Back in Paris, Misia introduced her friend Coco to well-known writers and artists from all over the world. Paris was the center of art at that time. Any new idea was welcome! It was a lively era that the French called "the crazy years"— *les années folles*!

Artists were experimenting in every field: in theatre and ballet, in literature and painting, and in the art of sculpture. Coco generously supported her artist friends with money.

Darling Coco

In 1924, Coco met one of the richest men in England, the Duke of Westminster.
He was tall, blonde and charming, and he was related to the British royal family.
But Coco loved him more for his natural personality and the simplicity of his
lifestyle. With him, she would enjoy horse riding through the English countryside,
sailing, and learning how to catch salmon!

England also meant experimenting with different fashion ideas. Coco discovered
British fabrics, such as tweed, which she used for her jackets and suits.

Villa with a sea view

Coco was 45 years old when, in 1928, she bought a real palace with a sea view in the south of France. The house was called *La Pausa*, and Coco had it remodeled according to her designs, which included a broad, white staircase. In its austerity and plainness, La Pausa was reminiscent of the orphanage in Aubazine. It was a beautiful house with whitewashed walls and a garden full of olive trees. Coco was able to relax there and enjoy a long break, along with her dog and friends.

31 Rue Cambon

For Coco Chanel, work remained the most
important thing of all. Her address in Paris,
31 Rue Cambon, was a multi-storied center of
life and work. Coco presented her collections
on the ground floor. The walls on this floor
were covered in mirrors, and columns shaped
the room. A curved staircase, which was also
covered in mirrors, led to a first floor that
had studios and private living quarters.

Coco's own apartment was beautifully decorated. A huge sofa adorned the main room. Hundreds of books by author and poet friends were littered about. Oriental screens divided the room, bronze lions guarded over it and lush bouquets of flowers filled it with their fragrance. The apartment was a universe full of memories and culture. Its elegant colors were beige, brown, white and black.

"J'aime la vie! I feel that to live
is a wonderful thing."

COCO CHANEL

Hello, Coco

Coco's success went beyond borders and oceans.
At the beginning of the 1930s, she was invited to New York
and Hollywood to dress American movie stars.

All women are Chanel

Coco Chanel not only designed clothes for women, she also gave them a style and a new silhouette. These clothes were for women who loved freedom, who worked and drove cars, and who felt liberated and self-confident.

Marlene Dietrich
Actor

Soon, there were Chanel women all over the world—young and old, full-time mothers and movie stars. Even Jackie Kennedy, the wife of American President John F. Kennedy, wore Chanel!

Jackie Kennedy
First Lady

"Fashion is in the air,
in the sky, on the streets"

COCO CHANEL

Gloria
Swanson

Actor

Romy
Schneider

Actor

Audrey Hepburn

Actor

Jewelry is chic

Coco wanted to give women something that they didn't already have. With this in mind, she invented fashion jewelry. These new jewelry designs didn't use real gemstones, and they were meant to be affordable. Coco created the pieces herself, assembling them from green and red stones, white pearls and crosses. She created necklaces, bracelets and broaches for dresses, jackets and hats.

Women not only wore Coco's chains around their neck. They also wore them across their shoulders, around their waists, on their backs and in their hair! Coco also encouraged them to wear many chains at once. Laying several chains on top of each other, crossed and worn long, could look very sophisticated.

"In order to be irreplaceable,
one has to be different."

COCO CHANEL

War, again

The Second World War erupted on September 1, 1939, when Germany, which was ruled by the National Socialists (the Nazis), invaded Poland. Germany conquered Paris in 1940, and France soon had to surrender. A painful period of occupation commenced. A large number of French people resisted the Nazis. They became part of the 'Résistance' movement, which helped the English and Americans in their struggle against the Nazis. There were, however, some French people who worked with the German occupiers—the so-called 'collaborators'.

Because of these dramatic events, Coco closed her stores. She also had a relationship with a German officer, whom she asked to free her nephew, André. André had been caught in the war and imprisoned in Germany.

In exile

Coco Chanel went through a confusing time after the war.
She was accused of having collaborated with the enemy.
Coco decided to leave Paris and move to Switzerland.

She took a long break, and her stores in France remained closed. Coco was rich, but she sorely missed her work and became very lonely. She read, went for walks and observed how fashion was changing as the years went by. She noticed other designers emerging and other styles evolving.

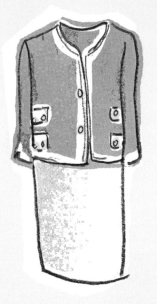

Coco is back!

When Coco returned to Paris in 1954, she was 71 years old, an age when most people have already retired. But for her, work was just as important as breathing air. She threw herself into a new adventure! In 1955, she designed a timeless garment for the active, modern woman: the Chanel dress suit.

This suit was a massive success, and it would go on to become a classic that every woman wished to have in her wardrobe. Once again, Coco proved her talent and instincts. She simply knew what women needed at a certain time. The tweed costume with its box-shaped little jacket came in thousands of colors and variations. It was simple and elegant at the same time—just like Coco Chanel!

Perfume
Chanel Nº 5

The most famous perfume

At the beginning of the 1920s, Coco Chanel, who was always looking to invent something new, had created perfume N° 5. Its fragrance of jasmine, rose and other flowers was unique. And the design of the simple, angular bottle with the single number 5 was equally successful!

Coco herself modeled perfume N° 5 in advertisements. She wore a long, black dress and leaned against a majestic fireplace.

This perfume was so original that Marylin Monroe, the famous American actor, along with every woman in the world, wanted to use Chanel N° 5. It became the world's most sold fragrance.

The quilted bag

But Chanel Nº 5 wasn't everything! Frustrated at not owning a handbag that she could sling over her shoulder to keep her hands free, Coco simply designed one herself. On February 2, 1955, she unveiled her angular bag in black, quilted leather with an adjustable chain.

This bag, called '2.55' after its release date, was practical because it could be carried by hand, on the arm or over the shoulder. It had several compartments inside and even a secret one for love letters! The 2.55 became instantly popular with women of every generation.

The 'little black dress'

Coco never forgot the need for women
to dress elegantly and, at the same time,
comfortably—whether they were out for an
evening at a restaurant or at the theatre. As
early as 1926, she had designed a very simple
model for a knee-length, neck-hugging dress.
This design eventually became known as the
'little black dress', and it is still available in
various cuts and materials to this day. Actors
and singers have made it famous the world
over. One of them was Audrey Hepburn,
who wore it in the film *Breakfast at Tiffany's*.
Even now, the little black dress stands
for simple elegance.

Farewell, Coco

Coco died on January 10, 1971, at the
age of 87. She had been living for quite a
while at the fashionable Ritz Hotel in Paris.

Her death left behind the image of an
elegant, emancipated and strong woman,
who never allowed the obstacles of her life
or the judgment of others discourage her.
Self-determined, Coco went her own way
and encouraged the generations that
followed, even to this day. She became
a role model for countless people.

Chanel forever

"Fashions fades,
only style remains
the same."

COCO CHANEL

The Chanel style is unique. It is stylish, comfortable and timeless.

The quilted leather bag 2.55

The straw hat (canotier)

Chanel N°5 perfume

The leather gloves

The lipstick

The pearl necklace

The tweed jacket

The powder case

The 'little black dress'

The cloche

The big sunglasses

Beige ballerina flats with round black tips

The 'must haves' from Chanel are classic garments and accessories. They all typify the Chanel brand.

Spectacular shows

Following the death of Coco Chanel,
fashion shows of the Chanel label
have become more and more
spectacular. They are gigantic and
magnificent, and they're more than
just a place to see and admire fashion.
They are staged like a play at the
theatre! The extraordinary sets, often
housed at the Paris Grand Palais,
are unique and hotly anticipated
every year. Chanel fashion shows
can feature artificial ice floes, majestic
golden lions, magnificent Parisian
street scenery, a meter-high Chanel
jacket or a huge passenger ship
about to set sail.

Catwalks

Chanel's fashion collection varies from season to
season—Spring/Summer and Autumn/Winter.
It may feature clothing you can find in the store,
which is produced in large quantities and can be
worn immediately. Or it may feature haute couture,
which is all about tailor-made products and
individual pieces that are luxurious and expensive.

At the fashion shows, models show off new creations by walking in single file, one after the other. This procession is called the 'catwalk'. The models walk by placing one foot directly in front of the other, just like cats. They sway their hips and almost glide past the admiring public.

The highlight at the end of the show sees the 'bride' of the show, followed by the fashion designer. Here you can see Karl Lagerfeld, who became artistic director of Chanel in 1983.

Coco Chanel BIOGRAPHY

August 19, 1883	Coco is born in Saumur and is baptized by the name of Gabrielle.
1895	Jeanne, Coco's mother, dies.
1895-1900	Life at the orphanage in Aubazine.
1900-1906	Trains as a dressmaker in Moulins; Gabrielle becomes 'Coco'.
1906	Coco lives at the chateau in Royallieu, north of Paris. Coco designs riding clothes for women.
c. 1907	Coco falls in love with Arthur 'Boy' Capel.
1910	Coco designs her take on the 'canotier' straw hat. The hat shop 'Chanel Modes' is opened in Paris.
1913	The Chanel boutique is opened in Deauville; Coco creates casual sailor outfits for women.
1914-1918	First World War
1915	The fashion house is opened in Biarritz.
1917	Coco discovers the boyish look for women, with the 'garçonne' short hair style.
1918	Haute couture in Paris
1919	Death of 'Boy'
1920s	Coco meets international artists in Paris. She creates Chanel N° 5, the brand label 'CC' and the little black dress.
1924-1931	Life in England.
1928	Coco acquires the villa *La Pausa* in the South of France. She extends and refurbishes the Paris fashion house at 31 Rue Cambon.
1930s	Coco dresses Hollywood. Fashion jewelry by Coco.
1939-1945	Second World War
1945	Exile in Switzerland.
1954	Return to Paris: Coco discovers the Chanel dress suit and the quilted leather bag '2.55'.
January 10, 1971	Coco dies in Paris.
Post-1971	'Chanel' lives on and remains one the most successful fashion brands in the world.

© 2022, Prestel Verlag, Munich · London · New York
A member of Penguin Random House Verlagsgruppe GmbH
Neumarkter Strasse 28 · 81673 Munich
© Text and illustrations: Isabel Pin

Library of Congress Control Number: 2022935031
A CIP catalogue record for this book is available from the British Library.

Editorial direction: Doris Kutschbach
Copyediting: Brad Finger
Design, layout and typesetting: Meike Sellier, Eching
Production management: Susanne Hermann
Separations: Reproline Mediateam, Munich
Printing and binding: TBB, a.s., Slovakia

Prestel Publishing compensates the CO_2 emissions produced from the making
of this book by supporting a reforestation project in Brazil. Find further
information on the project here: www.ClimatePartner.com/14044-1912-1001

Penguin Random House Verlagsgruppe FSC® N001967

ISBN 978-3-7913-7508-3
www.prestel.com

1980

1987

1990

2001